INSIGHT'S BIBLE COMPANION

PRACTICAL HELPS FOR BETTER STUDY

INSIGHT FOR LIVING

Anaheim, California

What did early manuscripts of the Bible look like?

The cover invites you to glimpse into the Bible as early readers saw it. On the left, examine a section of the ancient Hebrew text of Isaiah as preserved in the Dead Sea Scrolls. This entire manuscript, discovered in 1947 in a cave in Qumran, an area alongside the Dead Sea, was written on seventeen sheets of leather sewn together to form a continuous scroll twenty-four feet long. The Greek text, on the right, pictures a portion of a ninth-century manuscript of the gospel of John. The apostle John wrote this final gospel near the end of his life and the end of the first century. Early tradition cites that he penned it while in Ephesus on the western coast of modern Turkey.

In spite of persecution, neglect, and obscurity, God promises that His Word will be preserved. "The grass withers and the flower fall, but the word of our God stands forever" (Isaiah 40:8).

Insight's Bible Companion: Practical Helps for Better Study

Copyright © 1998 by Insight for Living

Published by:
Insight for Living • Post Office Box 69000 • Anaheim, California 92817-0900
www.insight.org

ISBN 1-57972-237-7

Unless otherwise identified, all Scripture references are from the Holy Bible, New International Version [NIV] © 1973, 1978, 1984 International Bible Society, used by permission of Zondervan Bible Publishers. Scripture taken from the New American Standard Bible [NASB], updated edition, copyright © The Lockman Foundation 1960, 1962, 1963, 1968, 1971, 1972, 1973, 1975, 1977, 1995. Used by permission.

Cover Image Credit: Hebrew image: from the book of Isaiah from the Dead Sea Scrolls, provided by the Ancient Manuscript Center, by permission of photographer Dr. John Trever. Greek script image: from a ninth-century copy of the gospel of John, provided by The Scriptorium, Center for Christian Antiquities.

Text and cover design by Gary V. Lett

Printed in the United States of America

Contents

> God didn't simply *think* His message. He didn't simply *speak* His message or reveal it in the clouds or communicate it through dreams to men and women in Biblical times. No, He saw to it that His Word was actually written down. He put it in the language of the people, so that people in all generations could read it and grasp its significance and be transformed by it. We're grateful we have a book that contains the very mind of our God — the Scriptures — in written form.
>
> Chuck Swindoll

And because God felt it was so important to give His Word to us, shouldn't we take time to investigate it, read and study it, and allow it to touch our lives?

With this *Practical Bible Companion* you will discover the *why, what,* and *how* concerning the Scriptures.

✔ *Why* can you have confidence in the Bible — that it is accurately God's Word?

✔ *What* is the subject of the Bible from cover to cover?

✔ *How* do you study God's Word personally?

You'll be given specifics, such as how to do a topical Bible study, a word study, and a character study; and supports, such as how an understanding of geography, literature, history, and archaeology enhance Bible study. Lastly, this *Companion* will guide you in digging deep for lasting guidance and encourage you to become a companion for others on their spiritual journeys.

INSIGHT'S
BIBLE
COMPANION

PRACTICAL HELPS
FOR
BETTER STUDY

1

THE
IMPORTANCE
OF
GOD'S
WORD

Why We Have Confidence in the Bible

b y   C h u c k   S w i n d o l l

Chuck Swindoll is the president of Dallas Theological Seminary and chairman of the board of Insight for Living.

What is your final authority in life? I mean, when you're cornered, when you're really up against it, when you're forced to face reality, upon what do you lean?

Before you answer too quickly, think about it for a few moments. When it comes to establishing a standard for morality, what's your guide? When you need an ethical compass to find your way out of an ethical jungle, where's north? When you're on a stormy, churning sea of emotions, which lighthouse shows you where to find the shore?

There can be no more reliable authority on earth than God's Word, the Bible. This timeless, trustworthy source of truth holds the key that unlocks life's mysteries. It alone provides us with the shelter we need in times of storm.

But we need to understand why. Why does this Book qualify as our final authority?

God's Word Is Truth

"Your word is truth," Jesus said as He prayed to the Father (John 17:17). Truth, real truth, truth you can rely on, truth that will never shrivel up or turn sour, truth that will never backfire or mislead, that's the truth in the Bible. That is what the Bible is about. That is why the Bible provides us with *the* constant and *the* needed support.

God's Book Is God's Voice

Scripture is "God's message." It is, in fact, "God's Word." The apostle Paul testified clearly to that truth in his first letter to the Thessalonians:

> And we also thank God continually because, when you received the word of God, which you heard from us, you accepted it not as the word of men, but as it actually is, the word of God, which is at work in you who believe. (1 Thess. 2:13)

Think of it this way: God's Book is, as it were, God's voice. If our Lord were to make Himself visible and return to earth and speak His message, it would be in keeping with the Bible. His message of truth would tie in exactly with what you see in Scripture — His opinion, His counsel, His commands, His desires, His warnings, His very heart, His very mind. When you rely on God's voice, His very message, you have a sure foundation; you have truth that can be trusted; you have power that imparts new life and releases grace by which you can grow in faith and commitment.

God's Word Will Endure

Do you realize there are only two eternal things on earth today? Only two: people and God's Word. Everything else will ultimately be burned up — everything else. Kind of sets your priorities straight, doesn't it? The stuff we place on the shelf, the things we put frames around, the trophies and whatnots we shine and love to show off, the things we're so proud of — it's all headed for the final bonfire (see 2 Pet. 3:7, 10 – 12). But not God's Book! Peter reminds us that the truth "stands forever" (1 Pet. 1:25). Grass will grow and then it will wither; flowers will bloom and then they will die. But God's written message, the truth, will abide forever. All His promises will be fulfilled; His redemptive truth cannot be annulled or changed; His powerful Word will accomplish what He desires and achieve the purpose for which He sent it (see Isa. 55:10 – 11). His Word will endure!

God's Word Is Inspired

But wait. Doesn't all this talk about the Bible lead to an important question that must be asked? The question goes like this: How can anyone get so excited about something that was written by men? We have no problem with the Giver of truth. He gave it . . . but wasn't the truth corrupted when He relayed it to earth through the hands and minds of sinful men?

This is the perfect moment for you to become acquainted with three doctrinal terms: *revelation, inspiration,* and *illumination. Revelation* occurred when God gave His truth. *Inspiration* occurred when the writers of Scripture received and recorded His truth. Today, when we understand and apply His truth, that's *illumination.*

The critical issue — your confidence in the Bible — is directly related to your confidence in its inspiration. How then can we be sure that God's Word is free from error, absolutely true, and therefore deserving of our complete trust? Paul provides great help in answering this question:

> All Scripture is God-breathed and is useful for teaching, rebuking, correcting and training in righteousness, so that the man of God may be thoroughly equipped for every good work. (2 Tim. 3:16 – 17)

When God revealed His truth for human writers to record, He "breathed out" His Word. When we dictate a letter to someone, we "breath out" a message and someone else types what we've said. But did

5

the writers of Scripture simply take dictation?

If you know much about the Bible, you realize that it was written by many different people with many different personalities. Peter doesn't sound like John; John doesn't sound like David. Somehow each writer's personality was preserved without corrupting the text with human weakness and error. That rules out the idea of dictation.

So how did God cause this to happen? Second Peter 1:21 gives us a further clue: "For prophecy never had its origin in the will of man, but men spoke from God as they were carried along by the Holy Spirit."

The English phrase "carried along" is translated from an ancient Greek nautical term *(phero)* describing ships at sea. When a ship was at the mercy of the winds, waves, and currents of the sea, it was "carried along" apart from its own power. That's the word used here. They raised, as it were, their sails, and the Holy Spirit filled them and they were "carried along" in the direction He desired.

God's Word Will Hold You Up

So our conclusion is this: In the Bible we have the preservation of a completely dependable, authoritative, inspired text. The question each of us must ask ourselves is this: Can I rely on it, especially when I go through those chaotic experiences in life? My answer, and I pray it is your answer, is this: absolutely and unreservedly! The wonderful thing about relying on God's Book is that it gives you stability. It gives you that deep sense of purpose and meaning. No other counsel will get you through the long haul. No other truth will help you stand firm in the storms of doubt and uncertainty. No other reality will give you strength for each day and deep hope for tomorrow. No other instruction has the power to give new meaning to your life.

Adapted from *The Living Insights Study Bible*, Charles R. Swindoll, gen. ed. (Grand Rapids, Mich.: Zondervan Publishing House, 1996), pp. 1312–1315.

The Incredible Story
of His Story

by   Larry   Sittig

Larry Sittig is a senior pastoral counselor with Insight for Living and a graduate of Dallas Theological Seminary.

Let's say that you are seated in your favorite armchair in a cozy living room on a wintry morning, your Bible on your lap, enjoying a leisurely time of intimacy with the Almighty. Okay, let's say you're huddled in the bathroom, hoping Mr. Rogers can keep the kids' attention for ten minutes so you can scurry through a few verses of Scripture and pick up some spiritual energy for the demanding day ahead. Or the rhythm of your Bible reading is marked by the clacking of the train's wheels on the track and by the chatter of fellow commuters. But how do you know, really know, that the words on the pages of your Bible are God's words for you?

Well, the Bible is "revelation" — God's truth given to us. It is God's inspiration — the Holy Spirit supernaturally moved human authors to write God's Word. That same Spirit now comes to us with His illumination. He opens up the life-changing truths of the Bible to spiritually reborn minds, allowing us to know and to grow.

But remember, almost two thousand years of human history have passed since the last time God's Spirit inspired a human author of Scripture. A two-millennia bridge connects its inspiration and your illumination. We need to examine that bridge and appreciate the marvels of its construction.

The ink was not even dry from the pens of the New Testament writers before Christians realized that Jesus was fulfilling a promise He had given to them: "The Counselor, the Holy Spirit, whom the Father will send in my name, will teach you all things and will remind you of everything I have said to you" (John 14:26). It must have been exciting to realize that God was inspiring documents to complement the Old Testament. God was continuing to unveil His masterwork.

These Christians, hungry for truth about their Savior, collected everything written about Him. When written documents about Jesus' unique person and life began to circulate among the earliest Christian churches, there immediately arose the conviction that God had inspired some of these writings, and they were to be accorded the same honor that Jesus had given to the Old Testament Scriptures. For instance, Paul calls a saying from Luke's gospel "Scripture," right along with a quote from Deuteronomy (1 Tim. 5:18). And the apostle Peter argues for the authority of Paul's writings as "Scriptures" (2 Pet. 3:15 – 16).

Just as apostles were only named from among those who had seen Jesus (Acts 1:21 – 26), so the church only considered authoritative those writings that had a very direct revelation of Jesus. As soon as the apostles began to pass off the scene, discussion began about which writings were inspired. But how could they discern between writings that were fully trustworthy and those that weren't? How could they know to reject documents that were fraudulent and heretical?

Nearly three centuries passed before these issues could be sorted out. Believers asked, Was this book or letter written either by an apostle or by someone like Luke or Mark who might be considered an official spokesperson for an apostle? Does it contain firsthand, reliable sayings, facts and truths about Jesus? Does it conform in *every respect* to the doctrine of the apostles, or is it tinged with heresy?

In the end, though, the question that determined the "canon"[1] of Scripture is this: Which writings has the Holy Spirit confirmed as God's Word? The remarkable consensus that was reached, regarding the thirty-nine books of the Old Testament and the twenty-seven books of the New Testament,[2] is testimony that God's Word is, indeed, recognizably "living and active," and "sharper than any double-edged sword" (Heb. 4:12).

Meanwhile, the Scriptures continued to be painstakingly hand copied until the printing press was developed fourteen centuries after Christ. The abundance of ancient manuscripts found scattered across the world gives us a huge base of data from which we can accurately reconstruct original documents. And the invaluable work of archaeologists and linguists gives today's Bible scholars a finer set of tools for accurate translation than the church has ever possessed. Therefore, we can be confident that our Bibles today have nearly the exact wording, and undoubtedly the same message, that flowed from the Spirit's heart through the apostles' minds and pens.

And what a debt of gratitude we owe to those who have taken the relay of God's Word in their generation and carried it to the next! What stories could be told! We honor those who handed over their copies of Christian writings to the pagan authorities of the Roman Empire, but would die before delivering their copies of Holy Scripture. We honor those medieval monks who disdained honor, pleasure, and adventure to spend their lives copying the biblical manuscripts with absolute fidelity. We honor those who have obeyed God rather than men as they have studied, translated, printed, and distributed the Bible at great personal

---

1. A canon is a standard of measure. The term has come to mean the group of writings that believers agree meet up to the standard of divine inspiration.

2. Roman Catholics and Eastern Orthodox include in the Old Testament certain additions called the Apocrypha that the Protestant Reformers considered to be of devotional value, but not inspired by God.

sacrifice and under fierce persecution. We honor those as well who today give their lives to put God's Word into the heart language of remote people groups scattered in the jungles, villages, and cities of the world.

Do you see the hand of God in the history of His Story? In all this, we can see God's faithfulness and persistence in building that bridge for His Word to all peoples of the world. Reflecting on God's powerful work to preserve and transmit His Word for us, we are moved to three important commitments.

✔ **To depend upon God's Word.** To regard it as uniquely valuable, powerful, and authoritative.

✔ **To obey God's Word.** To give it the supreme honor of a life devoted to learning from it and practicing, in the Spirit's strength, whatever it demands.

✔ **To give out God's Word.** To stand with those who promote Bible translation, Bible distribution, and Bible teaching around the world.

That way, God's masterwork will continue its masterful work in and through us.

2

JESUS
CHRIST
THROUGHOUT
THE
SCRIPTURES

Jesus Christ:
The Story of Scripture

b y   G a r y   M a t l a c k

Gary Matlack, a graduate of Dallas Theological Seminary, is director of educational ministries at Insight for Living.

"'The Greatest Story Ever Told' — this title," writes theologian Edmund Clowney, "has been used for the Bible, and with good reason. The Bible is the greatest storybook, not just because it is full of wonderful stories, but because it tells one *great* story, the story of Jesus."[1]

The *whole* Bible tells the story of Jesus? Doesn't His story begin in the first chapter of Matthew? It is there, after all, and it's in the second chapter of Luke, that we read of Christ's incarnation.

True, but the opening genealogy in Matthew reminds us that God had been planning the birth of our Savior long before that blessed day in Bethlehem. So we must go farther back — to the Old Testament — to find the story's beginning.

Perhaps Isaiah was the first to tell us of the coming Redeemer, when he wrote:

---

1. Edmund P. Clowney, *The Unfolding Mystery: Discovering Christ in the Old Testament* (Colorado Springs, Colo.: NavPress, 1988), p. 9.

> We all, like sheep, have gone astray,
>> each of us has turned to his own way;
> and the Lord has laid on him
>> the iniquity of us all. (Isa. 53:6)

The prophet, who had seen God's covenant people consistently reject Him, wrote of a Substitute who would pay for their sin with His own life. This idea of atonement, however, predates even Isaiah, so we must go back even further.

How about Exodus 12, where the blood of the Passover lamb shielded the Hebrews from God's wrath as He judged Egypt? Was this the first foreshadowing of Christ's death? Not quite. We must travel further still — all the way back to Genesis 3:15:

> "And I will put enmity
>> between you and the woman,
>> and between your offspring and hers;
> he will crush your head,
>> and you will strike his heel."

This passage foretells Eve's offspring, Christ Himself, who would suffer on the cross before securing victory over Satan.

You can't go back much further than Genesis. The apostle Paul, however, tells us that the story of redemption began even before the book of beginnings.

> Praise be to the God and Father of our Lord Jesus Christ, who has blessed us in the heavenly realms with every spiritual blessing in Christ. For he chose us in him before the creation of the world to be holy and blameless in his sight. In love he predestined us to be

> adopted as his sons through Jesus Christ, in accordance with his pleasure and will — to the praise of his glorious grace, which he has freely given us in the One he loves. (Eph. 1:3 – 6)

Amazing! Before God ever created the world, He chose us to be His own in Christ Jesus. So the glorious story of redemption actually began in the mind of God in eternity past. He loved us — and chose us — before He made us. And His Word, from Genesis to Revelation, reveals His unfolding plan to bring wayward humanity close to Himself through the blood of His dear Son.

The Bible is indeed the greatest story ever told. Not just because of how it reads, but because of who it reveals: the Lord Jesus Christ Himself.

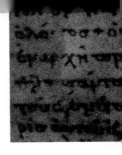

Jesus Christ: The Focal Point of History

b y   T o m   K i m b e r

Tom Kimber is a graduate of Talbot School of Theology and worked as an editor at Insight for Living

As you have read in the previous article, the Bible reveals Jesus Christ as the central character in the whole story from Genesis to Revelation. The following chart shows how Jesus is the central figure of history.

All the world over, people celebrate the entrance of God's Son into time and space, and the fulfillment of God's Word to us. Jesus is the dividing line of history, the centerpiece of Scripture, the focal point of God's message to men.

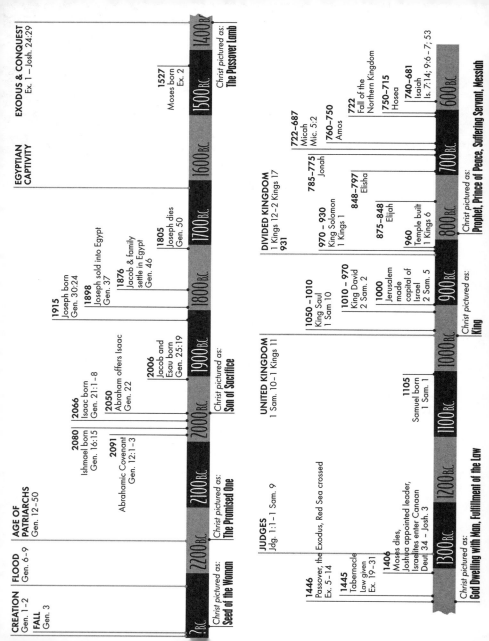

CREATION
Gen. 1–2

FALL
Gen. 3

FLOOD
Gen. 6–9

AGE OF PATRIARCHS
Gen. 12–50

EGYPTIAN CAPTIVITY

EXODUS & CONQUEST
Ex. 1 – Josh. 24:29

?B.C.

2200 B.C.

2100 B.C.

2000 B.C.

1900 B.C.

1800 B.C.

1700 B.C.

1600 B.C.

1500 B.C.

1400 B.C.

2091
Abrahamic Covenant
Gen. 12:1–3

2080
Ishmael born
Gen. 16:15

2066
Isaac born
Gen. 21:1–8

2050
Abraham offers Isaac
Gen. 22

2006
Jacob and Esau born
Gen. 25:19

1915
Joseph born
Gen. 30:24

1898
Joseph sold into Egypt
Gen. 37

1876
Jacob & family settle in Egypt
Gen. 46

1805
Joseph dies
Gen. 50

1527
Moses born
Ex. 2

Christ pictured as:
Seed of the Woman

Christ pictured as:
The Promised One

Christ pictured as:
Son of Sacrifice

Christ pictured as:
The Passover Lamb

JUDGES
Jdg. 1:1–1 Sam. 9

UNITED KINGDOM
1 Sam. 10–1 Kings 11

DIVIDED KINGDOM
1 Kings 12–2 Kings 17

1300 B.C.

1200 B.C.

1100 B.C.

1000 B.C.

900 B.C.

800 B.C.

700 B.C.

600 B.C.

1446
Passover, the Exodus, Red Sea crossed
Ex. 5–14

1445
Tabernacle
Law given
Ex. 19–31

1406
Moses dies,
Joshua appointed leader,
Israelites enter Canaan
Deut. 34 – Josh. 3

1105
Samuel born
1 Sam. 1

1050–1010
King Saul
1 Sam. 10

1010–970
King David
2 Sam. 2

1000
Jerusalem made capital of Israel
2 Sam. 5

970–930
King Solomon
1 Kings 1

960
Temple built
1 Kings 6

931

875–848
Elijah
1 Kings

848–797
Elisha

785–775
Jonah

760–750
Amos

750–715
Hosea

740–681
Isaiah
Is. 7:14; 9:6–7; 53

722–687
Micah
Mic. 5:2

722
Fall of the Northern Kingdom

Christ pictured as:
God Dwelling with Man, Fulfillment of the Law

Christ pictured as:
King

Christ pictured as:
Prophet, Prince of Peace, Suffering Servant, Messiah

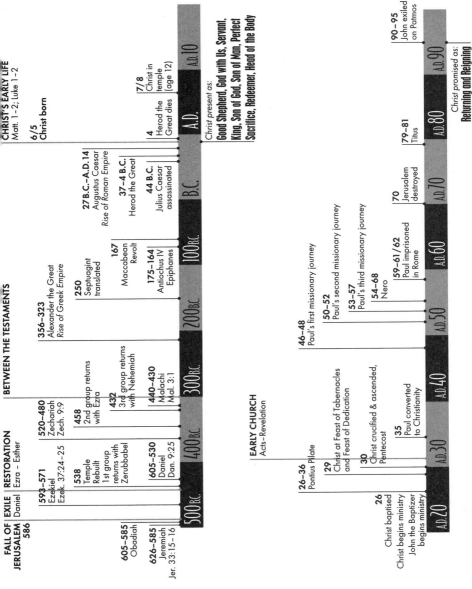

This time line is adapted from *The Living Insights Study Bible,* Charles R. Swindoll, gen. ed. (Grand Rapids, Mich.: Zondervan Publishing House, 1996).

3

UNDERSTANDING
THE
BACKGROUND
OF THE
BIBLE

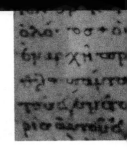

What's the Difference in Bible Translations?

b y   G a r y   M a t l a c k

Welcome to Decision Making 101. Here's your first assignment: choose a version of the Bible for your personal reading and study.

Oh, that's easy: the NIV. It's the most popular and the easiest to read, right? Well, except for *The Message.* Or is that a paraphrase? Although, I really appreciate the reverent language of the old NASB. King James? Well, it's a little rough to follow if you're not big on Shakespeare, but I hear it's more accurate. What's that? The *Jerusalem Bible?* Well, that sounds all right, but it seems like a long way to go just to buy a Bible. I mean, the plane ticket alone would. . . . Oh, sorry. Let's see, now, where were we? Oh, yes, Bible versions. . . .

Freedom of choice is a good thing. But it doesn't always make life simpler. Today's abundance of English translations and paraphrases requires us to educate ourselves in order to choose the version or versions that best fit our personal preferences and convictions.

Why are there so many English translations, anyway? Three main factors influence the number of translations available: the method of translation, the source of translation, and the historical development of the English language.

Difference 1: The Method of Translation

The two primary methods of translation are *formal equivalence* and *dynamic equivalence.* Formal equivalence can be described as a "word-for-word" translation. This method strives to render each word of the source material into one English word. Dynamic equivalence can be described as a "thought-for-thought" translation. This method aims to reproduce the meaning or idea behind a text. Therefore, it will often use several English words to represent one original word.

Then there's the *paraphrase,* which isn't really a translation. Rather than trying to render the original words into precise English equivalents, a paraphraser states in different words his understanding of the author's meaning. Beginning with an existing English version, he summarizes or elaborates where he deems necessary in order to communicate with the modern reader. Therefore, the paraphrase in effect becomes a compact commentary on Scripture.

Difference 2: The Translation Source

The manuscript source also helps explain the large number of translations. Since we don't have the original documents for the Old or New Testaments, translations are made from copies of the originals, or manuscripts. Without going into too much detail (you can find whole books written on this topic alone), there is an ongoing debate among scholars about which surviving manuscripts best reflect the original text. Some translators prefer *volume,* giving weight to groups of documents that contain the greatest number of copies of an original text. To others, *date* is the most important criteria; they prefer to translate from the oldest manuscripts, those closest to the original writings.

Difference 3: The Development of English

Finally, the development of the English language also helps us understand the proliferation of translations. The English language has gone through some major changes over the last few hundred years, and you can buy Bibles that reflect all stages of development— from Old English to Modern, from formal to colloquial. People prefer different translations for different reasons. Some, for example, use the NASB for detailed study, the NKJV for memorization, and the NIV or a paraphrase for casual reading.

The truth is that no single translation has everything— the most accurate reflection of the original, the easiest to read, etc. Yet the abundance of choices need not undermine our trust in the Bible. These translations reflect the desire of translators to put God's Word into the hands and hearts of people everywhere. And the fact that so many manuscripts exist actually supports the argument for original documents recorded by "men moved by the Holy Spirit" (2 Pet. 1:21 NASB).

The table below should help you get an idea of how a few major versions compare.

Type of translation	Publisher	Readability
New International Version (NIV)		
Dynamic equivalence	Zondervan	Easy to read; somewhat interpretive
New American Standard Bible (NASB)		
Formal equivalence	The Lockman Foundation	More of a word-for-word translation; less interpretive than NIV
New King James Version (NKJV)		
Formal equivalence	Thomas Nelson	More contemporary than the old King James, but preserves its reverent feel
The Living Bible (LB)		
Paraphrase	Tyndale House	Easy to read, but not recommended for serious study
The Message (the New Testament and selected Old Testament books)		
Paraphrase	NavPress	Very colloquial; contains informative and insightful introductions to Bible books

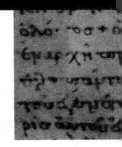

Understanding the Setting of God's Masterwork

by   T o m   K i m b e r

Before he ever puts his pen to the paper, a good playwright takes time to carefully assemble the elements of his drama: characters, conflict, story . . . and setting. Like the master playwright that He is, God set every event in the Bible in a particular place, at a particular time, among a particular group of people. The land became the stage on which the drama of redemption unfolded, and continues to unfold.

God did not convey His message through abstract philosophy, but through the vivid accounts of farmers and sheep and goat herders — people of the land. Scripture is rich with references to specific plants, landscapes, and climate — all working together to shape and express its message.

Though just a tiny dot on the world map, no plot of land has played a larger role in the history of man than Israel has. Therefore, the more we allow this unique land to teach us, the more alive the Bible becomes, and the better we understand its meaning.

As you follow the movement of God's drama, take time to examine the elements of the setting, down to the very details of the picture. How does a study of geography help us understand the Bible?

First, it provides a fuller understanding of the text. Living in the Promised Land is an act of faith. This simple fact is demonstrated in Deuteronomy 11:10–17. Understanding Israel's semi-arid climate, one quickly realizes the people's dependence on God to send the life-giving rains each year in their season.

Jesus often drew illustrations from familiar local scenes in order to make His point. In His Sermon on the Mount, it's easy to envision Jesus' gesturing to one scene after another. No doubt a flock of migratory birds sweeping up this enormous rift valley from Africa prompted Jesus to say, "Look at the birds of the air." Then, in the next breath, He looked at the hillsides blanketed in flowers and urged, "Observe the lilies of the field." Israel is second only to Switzerland in its display of wildflowers in the spring.

Jesus summarized that anyone who obeyed was like a wise man who built his house on the rock, rather than the sand. Probably some in the crowd were from Bethsaida, a town just below them where the Jordan River meets the Sea of Galilee. In summer, the dirt there is as hard as rock. But the winter rains cause the river and sea to rise and wash away the alluvial sand. Beneath this crust is a layer of bedrock. The wise man sweats and digs and picks away at that hard sandy crust to the bedrock underneath. Such an insight can change the point of the text. It suddenly becomes an issue not of *where* to build, but *how* to build.

Second, it helps confirm the accuracy of the text. Jesus begins His parable of the Good Samaritan with the words, "A certain man was going down from Jerusalem to Jericho." Traveling from Jerusalem's loca-tion atop Mount Zion, this unfortunate man headed steadily downward in elevation to Jericho, one of the lowest cities on the face of the earth, at the north end of the Dead Sea.

The same road is referred to in Luke 19. It is easy to follow the path Jesus took into Jerusalem as He faced His final days on earth. Again, coming from Jericho he was "ascending to Jerusalem" (Luke 19:28, NASB) approaching the villages of Bethphage and Bethany, both still located on the same road Jesus would have walked on His final approach into the city. Such geographical detail helps confirm the accuracy of Scripture.

Third, it brings the text to life. When I was a child in Sunday school, I loved the story of David and Goliath. What ten-year-old doesn't? First Samuel 17 gives the physical description of the battle site. But imagine standing on the hill looking down into the valley. There's a little brook on one side, and two large hills facing each other, and a broad green valley in between. When I stood there with my ten-year-old boy, I thought, "Wow, this is where it happened! David came from over there, picked up his stones from that creek there, and walked to this point here, and the giant was standing there."

The setting itself breathes life into the text. Suddenly, it's not a "once upon a time" kind of tale . . . it's real flesh and blood, facing the battles, trials, and tests of faith that you and I face right here and now.

In Luke 19:40, Jesus told the Pharisees on His triumphal entry into Jerusalem that if the people were hushed, the very stones would cry out. Sometimes it seems if you listen hard enough you can hear those stones and fields and hills and deserts tell a story that you and I can only imagine.

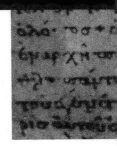

A Look between the Testaments

b y   G a r y   M a t l a c k

"The silent years."

That's how historians refer to the four-hundred-year historical bridge that connects the Old and New Testaments. But the phrase is actually somewhat of a misnomer.

Though the period was silent in terms of revelation — no prophet spoke during this time — it was anything but silent in terms of preparation. As author David O'Brien writes, "The events, literature and social forces of these years would shape the world of the [New Testament]." [1]

The New Testament World Takes Shape

During this intertestamental period, both Greece and Rome held the reins of world power. The Septuagint (the Greek translation of the Old Testament), the Dead Sea Scrolls, and the Apocrypha were written. The synagogues became the regular Jewish assembly for prayer and worship

---

1. David O'Brien, "The Time between the Testaments," *The NIV Study Bible*, ed. Kenneth L. Barker and others (Grand Rapids, Mich.: Zondervan Bible Publishers, 1985), p. 1431.

and were well-established by Jesus' day. And Jewish society, due to a variety of influences, splintered into sects — the Essenes, Pharisees, and Sadducees.

Looking back on the events of this period, particularly the rise and fall of world powers, we can see that, though God's voice may have been at rest, His hands were busy building the stage upon which He would deliver His grandest, most eloquent, most moving speech — Jesus Christ, the Word made flesh.

Kingdoms of Earth and the Kingdom of Heaven

During Malachi's day (he wrote the last book of the Old Testament), the land of the Jews belonged to the Persian Empire. By the time we get to Matthew, though, Rome is in power. What happened in between?

The Grecian Empire

About a century after Malachi wrote his book, Alexander the Great's military machine rolled eastward across Asia Minor, eventually reaching Palestine and as far as Egypt.

Alexander dreamed of building a new world bonded together by Greek language and culture. This policy, known as Hellenization, eventually established common or *koine* Greek — the language of the New Testament. Unwittingly, Alexander was a tool in God's hand to prepare the world for the spread of the gospel.

By 332 B.C., Palestine had been absorbed into the expanding Greek kingdom. History shows that Alexander generally treated the Jews with benevolence, even allowing them a measure of self-rule.

Alexander the Great died in 323 B.C. at the age of thirty-three. For about the next 150 years, his successors played tug-of-war for the control of the empire — with Israel stuck in the middle. One of those successors, Antiochus IV Epiphanes (whose name means "God made manifest"), ruled from 175 – 164 B.C. An arrogant tyrant, he "attempted to consolidate his fading empire through a policy of radical Hellenization."[2]

Antiochus' goal was to eradicate Jewish religion. He set out to destroy all copies of the Torah and required offerings to the Greek god Zeus. His most famous atrocity was the erection of a statue of Zeus in the temple and the sacrifice of a pig on the altar.

His blasphemous policies triggered the Maccabean revolt (166 – 142 B.C.). This revolt gained independence for Judah until 63 B.C., when Rome, under General Pompey, dug its iron talons into Palestine.

The Roman Empire

Pompey "took Jerusalem after a three-month siege of the temple area, massacring priests in the performance of their duties and entering the Most Holy Place. This sacrilege began Roman rule in a way that Jews could neither forgive nor forget."[3]

Later, in 48 B.C., Pompey lost a power struggle to his former ally, Julius Caesar. Caesar held the reigns of power until 44 B.C., when he was assassinated. Subsequent wars and infighting brought Julius Caesar's adopted son, Octavian, to the throne.

Octavian, later called Augustus Caesar, founded the Pax Romana ("Roman Peace"), with its unprecedented prosperity and effective and orderly civil government.

Alexander's kingdom had brought cultural and linguistic cohesiveness to a formerly fragmented world. The kingdom of Caesar Augustus ushered in civil organization and peace. But it also brought conflict, for Augustus established the idea that Caesar was a god.

The stage was set, then, for the coming of a greater kingdom — the kingdom of God in the person of Jesus Christ. He would bring to humanity what no earthly ruler could give — forgiveness of sins, eternal life, and the revelation of the one true God.

---

2. O'Brien, "The Time between the Testaments," p. 1431.

3. O'Brien, "The Time between the Testaments," p. 1431.

Archaeology and the Bible

by Dr. Charlie Dyer

Charlie Dyer is assistant to the president and professor of Bible exposition at Dallas Theological Seminary.

What impressions come to mind when you hear the word "archaeology"? For some, the word conjures up romance and excitement — Indiana Jones galloping after the ark of the covenant. Others stifle yawns as they mentally wander through dusty museums filled with artifacts. Still others picture sun-bronzed archaeologists on a "dig" . . . gently brushing away dirt to expose treasures from the time of Abraham.

Archaeology as a science is a study of civilization's material culture that seeks to explain how people lived. Sometimes the work is exciting, most of the time it is tedious. But much of the archaeology done in the Middle East has helped us understand more clearly God's Word. Specifically, archaeology has helped us in three ways.

Archaeology Helps Interpret God's Word

Some archaeological finds have served as keys, unlocking the message of God's Word. Archaeologists discovered an ancient city in northern Syria named Ugarit. During the excavations they uncovered clay tablets containing stories about the god Baal and a stone monument to Baal. The tablets and the monument pictured Baal as the god of lightning and rain. He was the storm god responsible for bringing fertility to the land.

These archaeological discoveries helped us understand the ministry of Elijah. King Ahab of Israel "set up an altar for Baal in the temple of Baal that he built in Samaria" (1 Kings 16:32). God's response was to announce through Elijah, "As the Lord, the God of Israel, lives . . . there will be neither dew nor rain in the next few years except at my word" (17:1). God challenged Baal in the very area that was supposedly Baal's strength — the ability to bring rain.

Several drought-filled years later Elijah summoned Baal's prophets to a contest at Mount Carmel. Each group would prepare a sacrifice. "Then you call on the name of your god, and I will call on the name of the Lord. The god who answers by fire — he is God" (18:24). This seemed fair . . . since Baal was the god of lightning.

The archaeological finds at Ugarit help us understand why rain and fire are so important in God's contest with Baal. God's withholding of rain — and His sending fire from heaven to consume the sacrifice — are clear proofs that He, not Baal, deserved Israel's worship as God.

Archaeology Helps Illuminate God's Word

I vividly remember the first time I ever watched color television. A friend invited me to watch the Rose Bowl parade. Seeing the parade in color brought out details that had been lost on our black-and-white television at home. Archaeology can have the same effect on the Bible, highlighting details that would otherwise not be so obvious.

In the book of Ephesians, Paul wrote to Gentiles who were once "separate from Christ, excluded from citizenship in Israel and foreigners to the covenants of promise, without hope and without God in the world" (Eph. 2:12). Paul announced that Christ's death "destroyed the barrier, the dividing wall of hostility" (v. 14) that had excluded Gentiles from God's place of blessing.

Paul's illustration comes from the temple that stood in Jerusalem in his day. Gentiles were permitted into the outer court, but they were restricted from entering any further into the temple by a low wall, or balustrade, that marked the limit of their access to God. In 1935 a portion of a stone from this wall was discovered. An inscription on the stone warned Gentiles of the severe consequences of trying to go beyond this barrier. "No foreigner may enter within the balustrade and enclosure around the temple area. Anyone caught doing so will bear the responsibility for his own ensuing death."

This archaeological discovery adds vividness and depth to Paul's words. The barrier in the temple was a visible reminder that Gentiles had been excluded from the blessings God had given to His people, Israel. But Christ's death on the cross shattered the barrier and gave all believers "access to the Father by one Spirit" (v. 18).

Archaeology Helps Validate God's Word

Sometimes archaeology has helped defend the accuracy and reliability of God's Word. Many scholars have criticized the unity of the Book of Isaiah. Instead of accepting Isaiah as the author, they assign different parts of the book to multiple authors over several centuries. They assume Isaiah 1 – 39 and Isaiah 40 – 66 were written at different times and were joined together at a later date.

In 1947 a Bedouin shepherd found several ancient manuscripts on the northwestern shore of the Dead Sea. These manuscripts became known as the Dead Sea Scrolls. The final collection contained portions of nearly every book of the Old Testament. The scrolls were one thousand years older than any previously known copies of the Old Testament.

Scholars were excited because they hoped these scrolls would shed light on their theories as to how the "pieces" of the Old Testament had come together. Two copies of the Book of Isaiah were discovered in one cave. One scroll was in almost perfect condition. Would this archaeological find prove, or disprove, the unity of the Book of Isaiah?

In this manuscript, the text of Isaiah 39 ends one line from the bottom of a column. Isaiah 40 begins on the very next line — with absolutely no evidence of any division! This archaeological discovery supports the unity of the Book of Isaiah.

And in conclusion . . .

The Bible does not depend on archaeology for its authority. It is authoritative because God is the author. But archaeology can help interpret, illuminate, and validate God's Word. It's encouraging to know archaeological finds support biblical facts.

Though written four decades ago, the words of the great archaeologist Nelson Glueck still ring true. "As a matter of fact, however, it may be stated categorically that no archaeological discovery has ever controverted a Biblical reference. Scores of archaeological findings have been made which confirm in clear outline or in exact detail historical statements in the Bible." [1]

Archaeology helps confirm God's masterpiece!

---

1. Nelson Glueck, *Rivers in the Desert* (New York, N.Y.: Farrar, Straus and Cudahy, 1959), p. 31.

_4_

STUDYING
AND
APPLYING
GOD'S
WORD

Finding Direction at the Crossroads of Life

by   B r y c e   K l a b u n d e

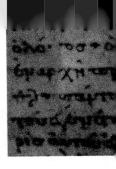

Bryce Klabunde, a graduate of Dallas Theological Seminary, joined Insight for Living as a study guide writer in 1991 and now serves as a pastoral counselor.

Turning points. They are life's transition periods — the curves in the road that take us off the familiar highway and down new and unknown roads. Maybe you're traveling down one right now.

Graduation, a new career, marriage, parenthood, an empty nest . . . all these life changes can leave us searching for the right map that will lead us to our destination.

God often uses these seasons of transition to teach us valuable lessons. So rather than fight them, a better approach is to lean into the curves . . . and hang on to something solid, changeless, and certain. That something is God's Word.

How does Scripture help us during times of change? Three thoughts will help you gain God's perspective during unstable times.

First, don't wait until a crisis to find God's direction. A good driver keeps the map handy all along the way, and consults it regularly. We must do the same. We're much more likely to find direction in God's Word if we're familiar with it. That's why we must regularly spend time reading our Bibles.

The psalmist declares "Your testimonies also are my delight; They are my counselors" (Ps. 119:24 NASB). Later in the same chapter, he describes God's Word as a "lamp" and a "light" (v. 105). This kind of illumination and counsel comes through regular meeting with God in His Word.

Second, find reassurance in the stability of God's character. James tells us that in God there is "no variation, or shifting shadow" (1:17). Even though the world may change, turning points may come and go, God never changes. We can count on Him to remain constant even though everything in life is in a constant state of flux.

Because God is our one constant, we can find stability in Him when everything around us is unstable. And the better we know Him, the tighter we can cling to Him during times of unrest or insecurity.

David described God as his "strength," "rock," "fortress," "deliverer," "refuge," "shield," "salvation," and "stronghold" (18:1–2). How could David be so confident? Because he knew Him personally and trusted Him completely.

Third, trust the Holy Spirit to be your teacher. One of the roles of the Spirit is to guide us "into all truth" (John 16:13). That's why it's always helpful to begin any study with the prayer of the psalmist: "Open my eyes that I may behold Wonderful things from Your law" (Ps. 119:18 NASB).

Often in stressful times, a single biblical truth seems to leap from God's heart into ours. "That's it!" we exclaim. We find a respite from our anxieties in one profoundly personal passage.

Corrie ten Boom endured the horrors of a Nazi concentration camp and, later, a debilitating stroke. A simple phrase strengthened her: "My times are in your hands" (31:15). For D. L. Moody, the familiar line of John 3:16 released him from his long-held fear of God's wrath: "For God so *loved* the world" (emphasis added).

Through the turning points in your life, as well as the smooth, familiar stretches of highway, God may be leading you to eternal treasure in His Word. If you're feeling anxious today, look there for direction and relief.

Every turning point is an opportunity to know God better and grow more like His Son. Allow Him to teach you. Here are a few pointers that will help make that happen.

✔ Take time to quiet yourself before God. Ask Him to be your teacher.

✔ Trace your path and God's faithfulness through the discipline of journaling.

✔ Immediately apply any truths you discover.

Any trip is better when we share it with a good companion. The Lord wants to be there not only in the miles of rough road . . . but in the scenic stretches as well.

God's Masterwork ...
a Treasure Worth Finding

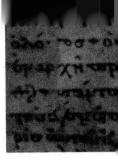

b y   W i l   L u c e

Wil Luce, a graduate of Dallas Theological Seminary, is an IFL pastoral counselor ministering especially to prison inmates.

The Bible — the very words and wisdom of God. What an incredible thought. And not the theoretical sort of wisdom intended to merely raise our IQ a few notches. It is practical stuff geared to show us how to live our lives successfully. Nothing in this world is of greater value or of more importance than the truth of this book. That is why Solomon writes:

> If you seek her as silver,
> And search for her as for hidden treasures;
> Then you will discern the fear of the Lord,
> And discover the knowledge of God.
> (Prov. 2:4 – 5 NASB)

Here is the wisdom we need to let us know when we are moving in the wrong direction, show us how to get back on track, and teach us how to live as God intended (see 2 Tim. 3:16 – 17). And since God is the author, we can be certain His Word is reliable and true.

So why don't we dig into Bible study more than we do? Possibly because our attempts have proven less than spectacular. While we see others hitting the mother lode of spiritual discovery, we feel that we've come up with little more than fool's gold. We may begin our quest with great enthusiasm, but it isn't long before disappointment and discouragement can set in. Somehow our efforts often don't meet our expectations.

If this describes your experience, take heart. By adding a few simple skills to your repertoire, Bible study can become the great experience you have heard others talk about. Let's look at a few ideas that will enrich the time you spend in God's Word.

Be Consistent

It's unwise to load up our bodies with a huge meal, then go for a week or two without food. The same is true spiritually. Regularity and consistency are critical. Here are some ideas that might help.

✔ **Pick a time when you are least likely to be interrupted.** Then, discipline yourself to keep the appointment, even when you don't feel like it.

✔ **Study at the same place each time, and stay there.** This will help your mind shift into a Bible study mode more quickly.

✔ **Keep everything you need right at hand.** Bible, study books, devotionals, pen, and paper should be within reach.

✔ **Ask God to give you understanding.** The Holy Spirit is the ultimate teacher, and He will lead you into all truth.

Be Methodical

Without a plan, you'll just be turning shovelfuls of empty dirt. You have to know *where* and *how* to dig, as well as *what* you're looking for. Begin by selecting a passage of interest to you. No matter which passage you begin with, you need that plan. How do you decide *where* to dig?

A good way to approach the New Testament is to begin with one of the four gospels, perhaps John. Then move through the transitional book of Acts, spend some time in the doctrinal book of Romans, and then the very practical letter to the Galatians. Later consider the difficult teachings of James and then tackle Hebrews and 1 John. Now you can return to one of the other three gospels and proceed from there to pick up some of the books you missed the first time through. Leave Revelation until you have a pretty good grasp of the rest of the Bible. Revelation might be seen as the Grand Central Station of Scripture where everything comes together. To understand it well, a knowledge of all that came before is needed.

So don't forget about the Old Testament. The New Testament has its roots in that part of the Bible. Frequently it portrays New Testament truth in illustrative form. The historical books, Genesis through Esther, can be followed chronologically for study purposes. For balance's sake, intersperse one of the poetical books of Job through Song of Solomon and include some prophetic books from time to time as well.

Don't feel bound by these recommendations. The Holy Spirit may prompt you to a different order because of specific issues that surface during the course of your studies. Consider these as suggestions.

Once you've decided where to dig, you need to know *how* to dig. Read your passage through prayerfully several times and ask yourself three questions about each verse.

✔ **First, what does it say?** This is observation. Be sure you understand the meanings of words. Try and uncover the who, what, when, where, why, and how of the passage.

✔ **Second, what does it mean?** This is interpretation. Once you understand the words, you can form them into deeper thoughts and teachings. Try and discover what it meant to the original audience. Enter into their world, their culture, their land, and their time.

✔ **Third, what does it mean to me?** This is application. By now, you should begin to see a key truth emerging. When you begin to understand the main point, you can apply it to your life.

A book that wonderfully develops this even more is *Living by the Book* by Howard and William Hendricks.

Be Thorough

What looks like a worthless dirt clod might conceal a valuable gold nugget. So don't overlook the details within the major themes of a passage. Invest in a few resources. A good study Bible is a great place to begin. These contain abbreviated libraries of information right with the text of Scripture. In addition, you'll want to have a good concordance and a Bible dictionary. Later, you can add a couple of one-volume commentaries on the entire Bible.

So how do you find those gold nuggets? Follow the techniques of observation, interpretation, and application. Write down both your questions and your answers. Glean as much information and understanding of the passage in this way before consulting what others have written. Use your dictionary and your concordance for better word understanding, but don't turn to the commentaries until you have exhausted your capacity to discern the meaning on your own. Then turn to the commentaries to verify and/or correct the conclusions to which you have come.

Now go ahead, grab your gear, and get ready to dig in and explore the hidden reaches of biblical discovery! It's a great sign of spiritual maturity and an indication that you're growing in your walk with the Lord as you uncover for yourself the priceless gems of biblical truth waiting to be found.

Discovering the Characters in the Greatest Story Ever Told

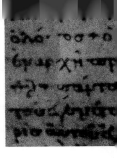

by Barb Peil

Barb Peil is a graduate of Dallas Theological Seminary and has been a writer at Insight for Living since 1994.

HOW TO STUDY A BIBLE CHARACTER

God, in His inspired Word, is the greatest storyteller of all time. With narratives like this that begin, "In the land of Uz there lived a man . . ." (Job 1:1), we are plucked out of our world and dropped into another. Suddenly we're in a different time and culture, and yet the characters we meet face challenges, disappointments, relationships, and crises of faith like ours. As we study their lives, they emerge from the two-dimensional storybook world to become real flesh-and-blood. Their characters become living models of faith (read Hebrews 11), and no matter how many times we read their stories, we see afresh God working in and through individual lives — no matter the time or place.

A part of immersing ourselves in an individual's life is seeing the world through their eyes. Observe every detail available about the political, geographical, and religious climate of their time. Then examine their personalities, relationships, and conflict. The better we understand their world, the more accurately and vividly we'll see God at work in their lives.

Learn about your character's world:

✔ Where did this person live? When Joseph's brothers betrayed him, they were in a remote region near open pits and a caravan route.

✔ When did this person live? Jonah's fear becomes clearer when we know he lived during the height of Nineveh's cruelty and terrorism.

✔ What attitudes, beliefs, and customs prevailed in the world at this time? As Jews in Moab, Naomi's family felt the terror and suspense of living in a racially hostile land, as perhaps a Jewish family would have felt living in Germany in 1939.

Use every relevant detail in the story to get to know their personality and character:

✔ What do you know about their physical appearance?

✔ How do other characters respond to them?

✔ What are their recorded thoughts and words?

✔ What does their actions say about them?

✔ Are they mentioned elsewhere in Scripture? What do others say about them?

Identify the conflict that the person faces:

✔ Are they facing a direct offense to a moral or godly command like Daniel or Esther?

✔ Is there disharmony in their family like in Isaac's or Abigail's?

✔ Like with Peter or Jonah, does the battle rage within their own heart?

✔ Are they in a conflict with another character like David or Stephen?

✔ Are they struggling to trust God in life's ordinary events like the ones Martha and Ruth faced?

If we can see our own experiences in a character's tests of faith, the story has captured something universal about life and can serve as a model of a spiritual truth. The way they responded to tests of faith become pivotal to the development of their character. The same is true today.

✔ How is your test of faith similar to what they faced?

✔ What does the fact that God provided this character as an example say about His character?

✔ What does it say about your faith, trust, or obedience to God?

✔ What is a principle you can apply to your life?

As you answer the questions above, write down your answers and observations. Read Bible commentaries, handbooks, and books on the culture in Bible lands to discover more about the world of your character. Read other Scripture sections where this person is mentioned. Then draw parallels between the conflicts and lessons this person faced and the ones that you now encounter. In so doing, you will transform the "Once upon a time . . ." to "There once was a man or a woman who faced the same kind of test as I do . . . and God was faithful to them." After all, these stories are not just about people, but what God did to and through ordinary people like you and me. God is the hero of every story. Including yours.

Seeking Counsel from God's Word

b y   W e n d y   P e t e r s o n

Wendy Peterson has been with Insight for Living since 1986. Currently, she is senior editor and assistant writer of IFL study guides. She also serves as IFL's librarian.

HOW TO DO A TOPICAL BIBLE STUDY

God is so gracious to share His wise counsel with us! Through His Word and His Spirit's guidance, we can learn to follow His ways in all aspects of life.

But where do we start? The Bible can seem so vast, so impenetrable. A systematic, book-by-book study beginning at Genesis is an overwhelming task when we need God's particular word at this moment in our lives.

This is when choosing a theme — like money, anger, family relationships, justice, or helping the poor — can best bring us in touch with God's wisdom.

By tracing a single topic through Scripture, we integrate God's teaching throughout time and in a variety of settings. Exploring a subject from many different angles provides us with a more complete, well-rounded picture — and a more clear, comprehensive response.

Before we lay out the basics of how to do a thematic study, we need to keep before us a few things *not* to do. These "nots" will hold us in place, preventing loose interpretations of Scripture that would set us up for a long, hard fall.

A Few "Nots" to Tie around Your Finger

The Bible is not *a "quick-fix" book.* It is God's revelation of Himself, His purposes, His ways, His relationship with us. It reveals His saving grace through all time. Through His Word, God shows us the way of life and how He means life to be lived. Though the Bible may not specifically address all of our problems or answer all of our questions, it will help us draw near to the God who loves and cares for us through it all.

The Bible is not *here to support our agenda.* We dare not approach God's Word with our own aims in mind. That kind of study is less than open — and less than honest. Rather, we study to discover God's agenda. It's His will we're after, not our own.

The Bible is not *a collection of unrelated sayings.* Scripture is rooted in context — the material surrounding the passage. Jesus' words in Luke 14:26, for example, aren't about family relationships; they address the priority of Christ and discipleship. Understanding the context of a verse or passage, and its connection to the whole Bible, will keep us from taking literally what was meant figuratively and will anchor us in the author's original intent.

Tools for Your Study

A thematic study requires certain tools. These include (1) a reliable Bible version (such as NIV or NASB) with plenty of cross references; (2) a concordance that matches your Bible version; and (3) a topical Bible, such as *Nave's* or *The Handbook of Bible Application,* which can give you a head start since it has already arranged Scripture under a comprehensive variety of topics. A Bible dictionary and Bible encyclopedia also come in handy, as does a user-friendly systematic theology if you're studying a particular doctrine.

Getting Started

Now that we've fastened our "nots" and gathered our tools, let's see how to do a thematic study.

✔ **Pray.** Ask the Lord to guide you and help you be receptive to what He wants to teach you.

✔ **Brainstorm.** If you want to study God's perspective on money, for instance, some other words you'll want to look up in the concordance would be riches, wealth, or gold.

✔ **Focus.** After examining the Bible passages you've found, cull out the peripheral verses, and record the more direct ones.

✔ **Organize.** Note the difference between specific, direct teaching and a story from which you think through a conclusion. Group passages that make a similar point.

✔ **Meditate.** Read and reread the passages you've chosen, perhaps in different versions to expand your insight. What are they saying in context? Discover how separate passages connect, and ponder why God says the things He has said.

✔ **Write.** Make notes about what you find throughout the process. Also, when you jot down your references, summarize what the verses say and interpret what they mean. Record questions you have and any answers you find. Integrate what you learn by writing it down.

✔ **Apply.** Think through questions like, What does this teach about God's nature? His purpose? How will this work itself out in my life?

The Lord's wisdom "is more precious than rubies," Solomon tells us, and "nothing you desire can compare with her" (Prov. 3:15). Let's partake of His counsel, then — for we'll be immeasurably richer for it!

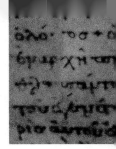

Understanding the Words of God's Masterwork

b y   T o m   K i m b e r

HOW TO DO A WORD STUDY

One of the greatest gifts God ever gave to us is His Word. It is a lamp to our feet and a light to our path. But there are times when the light seems dim, and the lamp appears to fade as we try and unravel the message before us.

Perhaps you've been amazed as others have looked into the pages of Scripture and seen things that you've never noticed before. Shades of meaning, nuances of language, relationships of words and ideas — these are all the subtle influences that carry the message of God's Word.

One of the best ways to decipher the truth of God's Word is to study the individual words that carry the message. As you learn to study these words, you'll discover new facets of scriptural truth you've never seen before as it explodes in brilliant colors and fascinating designs. Studying key words in Scripture can become one of the most valuable exercises you'll ever add to your Bible study.

Step one: Begin with a well-stocked toolbox. The most obvious tool is a good English translation of the Bible. The New American

Standard Bible (NASB), New International Version (NIV), and the New King James Version (NKJV) are some of the more common ones used today. Paraphrases like *The Living Bible* or *The Message* are good for other kinds of reading, but not for study.

Other helpful tools include a good English dictionary and a concordance in the same version of the Bible you're using. Even people who have never studied Greek and Hebrew can use *Vine's Expository Dictionary of Biblical Words*. A good Bible dictionary can also be helpful.

Now, let's see how to use these few tools in a simple word study.

Step two: Decide which key words need a closer look. Look for those words that carry the weight of the message. Are there any repeated words? Are there similar words used in different ways? Are there lists of words? Are there any words that you don't understand? In John 15, for example, Jesus repeats the word *abide* a number of times.

Step three: Be sure you understand the English meaning of the word. Use a good dictionary for a full definition of the word, noting the different meanings and alternate definitions, as well as the common, main definition.

Step four: Compare other translations. In the NIV, the word *abide* is translated "remain." These are two different translations of the same Greek word, each picking up on a different shade of the original meaning.

Step five: Use a concordance to see how the word is used in other passages. *Abide* is used several times throughout the New Testament. In the NASB, in 1 Corinthians 13:13, Paul tells us that faith, hope, and love "abide"; in 1 Peter 1:23, we're told that God's Word is "living and abiding." John 3:36 uses this word to describe God's wrath. As you look up these different verses, note any similarities and differences you can find.

Step six: Let the context be your guide. Again, in John 15, *abide* is used in reference to Jesus' teaching of the vines and the branches. What does His illustration tell us about this word? What do you know about vines and branches that can help you understand what it means to abide? Conversely, what negative teaching is there that illustrates what it means not to abide? What clues can you get from the passage?

Step seven: Draw on the wealth of available resources. One of the most helpful books you can use is *Vine's Expository Dictionary of Biblical Words.* Don't be intimidated by the Greek and Hebrew terms; this volume is actually quite easy to use. You'll discover that there are twelve different Greek words that are translated "abide." You'll also find which Greek word is used in John 15.

A good Bible dictionary may also help. The word *abide* won't be listed, but you can find information about vines and vineyards. This will not only help you understand the context, it will give you great insight into the culture, the times, and the people you're studying.

Step eight: Put all your information back together and look at the big picture. The goal is to understand Jesus' message. How do all the illustrations, definitions, and shades of meaning help you understand the beauty, fullness, and intent of "abiding"?

Always keep in mind that the objective is not to understand the complexities of Greek and Hebrew terms — it's to change our hearts and our lives. The more you understand the meaning of the individual words, the better you can understand and apply God's Word.

The Many Styles of God's Masterwork

by   B a r b   P e i l

VIEWING THE LITERARY FORMS IN SCRIPTURE

The story is told about a man who loved a woman so much that he spent years learning her language so he could tell her of his love. Night and day, he studied how to speak phrases she could understand, how to write with proper vocabulary and grammar so that she could read of his love for her. He did this because he understood that when you love someone, you want to communicate with them in the clearest and most accurate way possible. You want them to understand how you feel, so you communicate in the way most familiar to them.

God wrote His "letter of love," the Bible, to us with that same care. Infinite are the ways He could have communicated His story of redemption, but He chose to write it down in the ways more familiar to us.

Though it appears to be a single work, God's Word is actually a collection of works, written over hundreds of years, by a variety of authors in a number of styles and forms. Through the various literary techniques of the day, Scripture presents God's truth, while maintaining absolute theological, historical, and grammatical accuracy.

Many Styles — One Message

You already can guess many of the styles:

Psalms and Proverbs are essentially _____.
Poetry, you're right.

Romans, Corinthians, Thessalonians, and Timothy are all _____.
Letters, right again.

The majority of Genesis, Exodus, 1 and 2 Samuel, and Acts are

_____.

Narrative or stories about men and women and their relationships with God.

The Bible is a mixture of creative and expository (writing that seeks only to explain) styles, giving a complete picture of God's message of redemption. Seeing these forms is a full sensory experience — the analysis of word study, syntax, and theology, as well as the emotion of an individual's relationship with God. It's that human dimension of Scripture that invites us in, helping us to picture an omnipotent God in touch with His finite creation.

Picture David tending his flocks while composing songs on his lyre. His thoughts turn toward God's care for him. What passage naturally comes to mind? If you guessed Psalm 23, you've entered into the literature of the Bible. Through the vast stories about David's life and through an intimate look at his worship of God in the Psalms, we not only understand that David was a man after God's heart, but we've identified with him in his strengths and weaknesses as he walked with God.

Many Writers — A Common Theme

Other sections of the Bible come alive when you focus not only on *what* it says, but *how* it says it. The stories about Joseph, Esther, Noah, Abraham, Job, Elijah, Peter, Mary, Paul, and most significantly, Jesus, all invite us into their personal journeys of faith. Each **narrative** is enriched by character studies, theme, conflict, and resolution.

The figurative language, rhyming patterns, and structure throughout Psalms, Proverbs, and Song of Solomon personalize the significant theology found in biblical **poetry.**

Using the contemporary literary form of story-telling, Jesus effectively used **parables** in order to drive a significant decision of faith right to His listeners' hearts.

Jeremiah patterned Lamentations after a **funeral poem** that was normally recited for someone who had just died. Lamenting the tragic "death" of Jerusalem, Jeremiah used this style to express the survivor's feelings of sadness and loss.

Lamentations was also written, like Psalm 119, in an acrostic (alphabetical) style — an ancient poetic form intended to help people memorize large passages of Scripture.

Moses, perhaps leaning on his royal upbringing, modeled the structure of Deuteronomy after an ancient **suzerainty treaty,** typical of the second millennium B.C. When a king (a suzerain) made a treaty with a country, it usually contained six elements (which Deuteronomy parallels): a preamble, historical prologue, a call for wholehearted allegiance to the king, laws, witnesses, and blessings and curses related to their obedience.

Schooled by the most respected teachers in his day, Paul was a master of **debate.** Trace his logic through his letters, especially Romans. In Acts, you can follow his debates on Mars Hill, and other scenes of rhetoric. Stephen, in the Acts 7 sermon that predicated his death, developed a logical argument for the deity of Jesus Christ in typical debate rhetoric.

New Testament letters often mix varying styles of logic, poetry, prayer, and personal greetings.

Prophetic or **visionary literature,** such as sections of Isaiah, Daniel, and Revelation depict prophecy and the apocalypse in imaginative (image-creating) language, describing what is true, though not yet existing. These examples, plus many more found in Scripture, invite us to analyze and experience the truth of the Word through literary form.

A Personal Expression of Eternal Truth

The Word is incarnational — truth that comes alive. God was so committed to communicating with us in a way we could understand that His Word literally came alive. "The Word [Jesus] became flesh and lived for a while among us. We have seen his glory, the glory of the one and only Son, who came from the Father, full of grace and truth" (John 1:14).

Like the man who looked for every way possible to communicate with his beloved, God revealed Himself to us in a way we could understand — a way in which we could experience His truth and love.

Questions to Help You Understand the Literature of the Bible

✔ What style of writing is this passage? Is it figurative or concrete?

✔ Is this style unique to the original audience? What special meaning would it have had for them?

✔ What images does this writing create in my mind?

✔ How is God revealed in this section of Scripture? Is He a father? Lover? Friend? King?

✔ What can I learn about God's nature? God's dealing with man? Man's response?

✔ How does this writing express God's truth?

How to Prepare and Lead a Bible Study

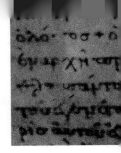

b y   G a r y   M a t l a c k

We've surveyed a lot of ground in *Insight's Bible Companion*. But there's a lot more rich truth below the surface just waiting to be discovered — if you're willing to drill and dig a little.

You might be wondering not only how to delve deeper into God's Word, but also how you can teach others to study the Scriptures. If so, here are some guidelines for developing a personal study plan and then imparting what you've learned.

Your Personal Study Plan

"What direction do I want to take?" That's the first question to ask in designing a plan. Does a particular theme, doctrine, book, historical period, or person stimulate your interest or stir your heart?

Maybe you want to fine-tune your picture of Creation or finish out your rough sketch of David or Mary. Perhaps you want to take a closer look at the church or examine how the gospel relates to the Mosaic Law. Are you a little weak on the life and ministry of Jesus? Then a parallel study of the gospels might be just the course of study.

Another question to help focus your direction is, "Where am I on my spiritual journey?" If you're a brand new Christian, for example, the book of Revelation is not the best point of departure. Books, however, that clearly present the person of Christ and the power of His gospel — John, Romans, Galatians — will stock you up for your spiritual journey, as well as prepare you for other, more difficult, books of the Bible.

Once you settle on a direction, estimate how long the study will take — a week, a month, a year — and carve out some time for regular study. You might prefer studying in daily, thirty-minute chunks or on two free weeknights — whatever works best for you. The important thing is to plan to do it. And be realistic. If you work ten hours a day and spend two hours on the road commuting, a four-hour-a-day study would be a little ambitious.

Here's another thought: Whenever you get an idea for a future study, write it down on an ongoing list. That way, you'll never run out of topics.

What's next? Well, just begin. Acquire any study aids you might need (and can afford) — study Bible, concordance, commentaries — and go for it. (See the suggested resources list at the end of this book.) You'll be amazed how much God teaches you through His Word in just a short time.

Preparing to Teach

Of course, once you start soaking in the life-changing water of God's Word, you might find that you want to pass it on to other thirsty souls. You don't necessarily need a pulpit to share the Scriptures with others, but you do need a plan.

First of all, if teaching is an area of giftedness or interest for you, be attentive to possible opportunities. Do you have Christian friends who were never grounded in the basics of the faith? Or maybe some of your non-Christian coworkers are itching to find out firsthand what the Bible is all about. If you're comfortable with tackling controversial topics such as abortion, euthanasia, and cloning, these also provide a framework for teaching.

Once you have a person or group of people who agree on the direction of study, put together a schedule. Are you going to meet once a week for three months straight? Or will you meet for six months with several breaks scattered throughout? How much material will you try to cover each time? The topic, urgency of study, and group dynamics will all influence the schedule.

What kind of format do you want? Are you going to do all the talking, or do you want lots of group interaction? You also need a time and place. During the lunch hour at work, at your home in the evenings, or on Sunday at church? Food or no food? One hour or two? "Prayer and share" time or strictly Bible study? You get the idea.

You'll also need to determine which supplemental materials, if any, the group will need — study aids, magazine articles, books, etc. Where can they acquire these? Can you provide them?

Most importantly, pray. Ask God to teach you first, to reveal whatever you need to change in your own life. Then ask Him to use you. Ask Him for clarity, accuracy, and wisdom as you help others tune in to His masterwork.

Additional Resources

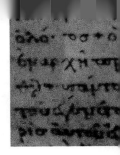

Archaeology

Blaiklock, Edward M. and R. K. Harrison, gen. ed. *New International Dictionary of Biblical Archaeology*. Grand Rapids, Mich.: Zondervan Publishing House, Regency Reference Library, 1983. A helpful resource to explain the archaeological findings related to the Bible.

Dyer, Charles H. and Gregory A. Hatteberg. *Christian Traveler's Guide to the Holy Land*. Nashville, Tenn.: Broadman and Holman Publishers, 1998. An easy-to-understand guide to the archaeological findings in Israel related to the Bible.

Bible Commentaries

Unger, Merril E. *The New Unger's Bible Handbook*. Chicago, Ill.: Moody Press, 1984. This book to gives background and other miscellaneous information not usually found in a formal commentary.

Walvoord, John F. and Roy B. Zuck. *The Bible Knowledge Commentary*. Wheaton, Ill.: Scripture Press Publications, Victor Books, 1985. A two-volume set based on the NIV text, covering both Old and New Testaments and written by either present or former faculty members of Dallas Theological Seminary.

Bible Dictionaries

Tenney, Merrill C., gen. ed. *The Zondervan Pictorial Bible Dictionary.* Grand Rapids, Mich.: Zondervan Publishing House, Regency, 1967. A one-volume dictionary providing quick access to information about the Bible in both words and pictures.

Vine, W. E., and others. *Vine's Expository Dictionary of Old and New Testament Words.* Nashville, Tenn.: Thomas Nelson Publishers, 1985. Easy-to-use dictionary of the Hebrew and Greek words used in the Bible.

Bible Study

Bruce, F. F. *The Canon of Scripture.* Downers Grove, Ill.: InterVarsity Press, 1988. This book traces origin of our canon from its beginnings to today.

————. "The Transmission and Translation of the Bible," in *The Expositor's Bible Commentary,* vol. 1, Frank E. Gaebelein gen. ed. Grand Rapids, Mich.: Zondervan Publishing House, 1979.

Fee, Gordon D. and Douglas Stuart. *How to Read the Bible for All Its Worth: A Guide to Understanding the Bible.* 2d ed. Grand Rapids, Mich.: Zondervan Publishing House, 1993. User friendly Bible study help, touching on characters, genre, background material, etc.

Hall, Terry. *How the Bible Became a Book.* Wheaton, Ill.: Victor Books, 1990. Good book, tracing the how the Scriptures came to be a book.

Hendricks, Howard G. and William D. Hendricks. *Living by the Book.*

Chicago, Ill.: Moody Press. 1991. A practical, easy-to-use guide on how to study the Bible.

Ryken, Leland. *How to Read the Bible as Literature.* Grand Rapids, Mich.: Zondervan Publishing House, Academie Books, 1984. A helpful book in understanding the various literary forms used in the Bible. For more in-depth reading, suggestions are given at the end of each chapter.

Stott, John R. W. *Understanding the Bible.* Grand Rapids, Mich.: Zondervan Publishing House, Lamplighter Books, 1979. Readable overview of the Bible with three chapters devoted to revelation, inspiration, and illumination.

Sproul, R. C. *Knowing Scripture.* Downers Grove, Ill.: InterVarsity Press, 1977. Among his helpful instructions is a clear discussion on why Scripture has practical application to our lives.

Geography

Baly, Denis. *The Geography of the Bible.* Rev. ed. New York, N.Y.: Harper and Row, 1974. A classic resource to study the geography of the Bible, especially the Old Testament.

Laney, J. Carl. *Baker's Concise Bible Atlas: A Geographical Survey of Bible History.* Grand Rapids, Mich.: Baker Book House, 1988. A helpful overview of biblical geography.

History

Matthews, Victor H. *Manners and Customs in the Bible.* Rev. ed. Peabody, Mass.: Hendrickson, 1991. Helpful tool for understanding the life and times of the people of the Bible.

Merrill, Eugene H. *Kingdom of Priests: A History of Old Testament Israel.*

Grand Rapids, Mich.: Baker Books, 1996. A good overview of the history of the Bible from a conservative theological position.

Study Bibles

The Handbook of Bible Application. ed. Neil S. Wilson. Wheaton, Ill.: Tyndale House Publishers, 1992.

The Living Insights Study Bible. ed. Charles R. Swindoll. Grand Rapids, Mich.: Zondervan Publishing House, 1996.

The NIV Study Bible. ed. Kenneth L. Barker and others. Grand Rapids, Mich.: Zondervan Publishing House, 1985.

The New Nave's Topical Bible. Orville J. Nave. Rev. ed. Grand Rapids, Mich.: Zondervan Publishing House, Regency Reference Library, 1969.

Insight for Living is the Bible-teaching ministry of Charles R. Swindoll. Our thirty-minute radio broadcast airs worldwide, almost 1,450 times daily. Along with broadcasting messages from God's Word, Insight for Living also supports our listeners in their personal and spiritual growth through such Christian resources and services as study guides, audiocassette series, and counseling by mail.